D0855712

LET'S VISIT
A Toy Factory

by Miriam Anne Bourne

photography by Michael Plunkett

Troll Associates

Library of Congress Cataloging in Publication Data

Bourne, Miriam Anne.
   Let's visit a toy factory.

   Summary: The reader visits a factory where the
step-by-step production of plastic cars and other
toys are made.
   1. Toy industry—Juvenile literature. [1. Toy
industry] I. Plunkett, Michael, ill. II. Title.
TS2301.T7B655   1988   688.7'2   87-3489
ISBN 0-8167-1159-3 (lib. bdg.)
ISBN 0-8167-1160-7 (pbk.)

Copyright © 1988 by Troll Associates, Mahwah, New Jersey

Printed in the United States of America.

10   9   8   7   6   5   4   3   2   1

The author and publisher wish to thank Gary Fortier, Wayne Charness and Hasbro, Inc. and Toys 'Я Us for their
generous assistance and cooperation.

Look at all those toys! Have you ever wondered where they come from? Do you wonder about how they are made? Let's visit a toy factory and find out.

This company makes millions of toys each year. Many of the toys are made of plastic parts. At the *molding factory,* pieces of each toy are molded into shape. Later, the toys will be assembled into cars, space creatures, and other playthings.

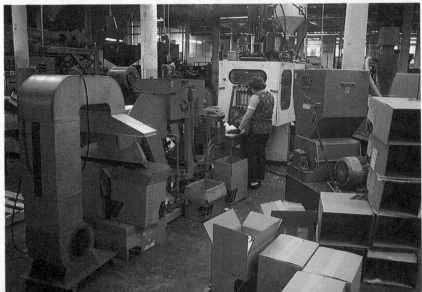

Before a new toy is made, someone invents it, or thinks of the idea. Next, an *artist* draws pictures of the toy and gives them to an engineer. The *engineer* draws plans of the molds which will make the parts of the toy. *Molds* shape plastic into toys, just as cookie cutters shape dough into cookies!

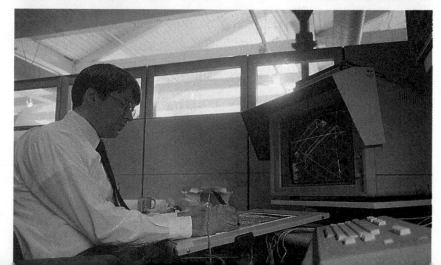

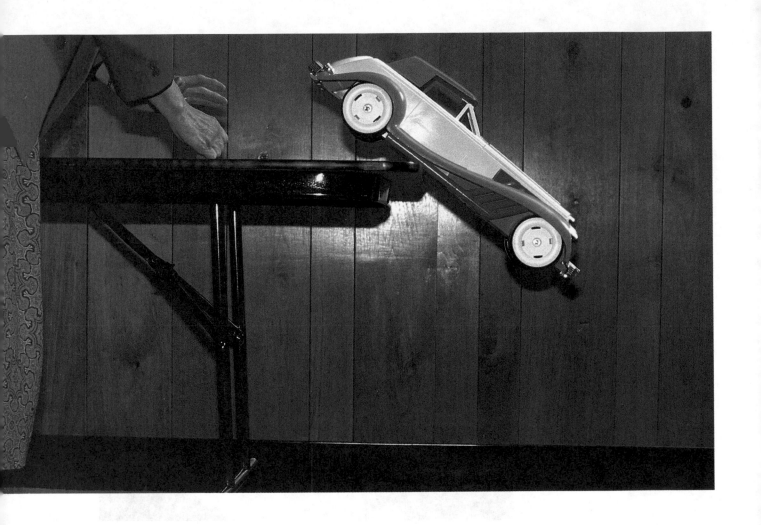

Sample toys are produced and then tested to
be sure that they are as safe as possible. One
of the ways that cars and trucks and toys with
wheels are tested is by rolling them off the
side of a table. They are *drop tested* six or seven
times to be sure they are durable. If they pass
their tests, production begins on the toys.

Most plastic playthings, like cars and trucks, begin as clear, *plastic pellets*. Freight trains carry the pellets to the molding factory. Here, they are stored in silos that hold as much as 200,000 pounds.

Colored powders are mixed with the pellets to get the right color for the toy. From vats, they are sucked into a machine where they are softened by heat. Soon, they melt together. Then they are shaped by a mold. The pink powdered pellets become the *chassis,* or bottom of the car.

Yellow pellets are melted together to form the body of the car. They, too, are shaped by a special mold at the factory. Plastic that isn't used is melted again to make other toys. Workers wear gloves in order to touch the hot plastic that comes out of the machines.

A much-loved cartoon character is molded in
another part of the factory. Once he is molded,
a worker must chip away all the extra plastic.
Leftover pieces of plastic are ground up and
used again to make more toys.

After they have been finely carved, each plastic figure is painted. A worker wipes away any smudges so that each little dog is perfect. Look closely at the big beagle ears and the long snout. Do you recognize this fellow? Do you know his name?

Finished parts of all the toys are then taken from the molding factory. They are brought to the *assembly factory*, where workers put them together. Cartons are unloaded and stacked like bricks along the aisles of the warehouse.

Fork lifts help workers carry the cartons to the assembly lines. Painted footprints show the workers where it is safe to walk. The factory is such a busy place—and it's very noisy, too. A fork-lift driver must honk his horn to let people know he's coming!

Toys are put together on an *assembly line*. A sixty-foot conveyor belt carries unfinished toys past the workers. As the pink chassis move along the belt, each worker adds a new part.

Holes are drilled for front bumpers and a radio. The FM radio comes from Hong Kong. A worker tests it to be sure that it works well, before it is screwed into the trunk.

The body of the car is snapped onto the chassis. Then it is glued into place. The factory is warm. Fans and tools clatter. Workers call out to one another—somebody needs more parts!

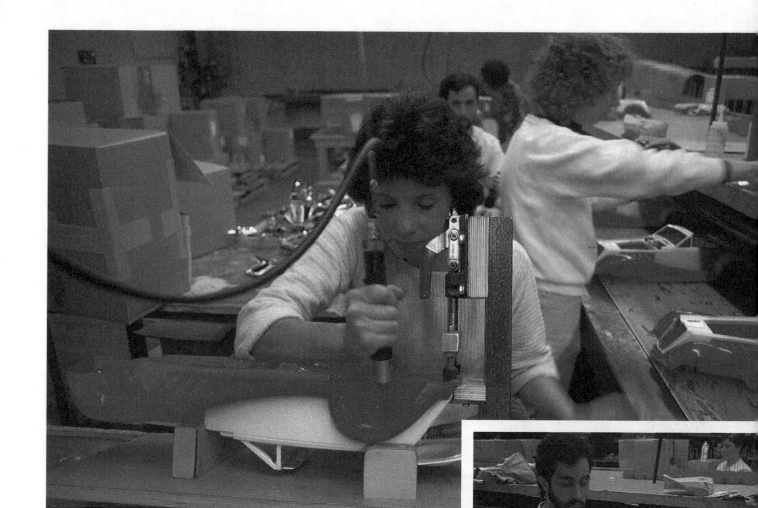

More holes are drilled with an air screwdriver. Now bumpers and a silver grill can be attached. Speed is important on an assembly line—each worker must move quickly, but not so fast that mistakes are made. In just 10 seconds another car will appear on the conveyor belt!

Right and left headlights are assembled next.
Then white walls are fastened to purple
wheels. The company hopes that the bright
colors of the car will appeal to the children.

Axles are added to hold the wheels. Then the wheels are attached. The windshield and roof are assembled next, but they are not attached to the car. Instructions are added to each toy to explain how to put them together.

Each car is wrapped in a plastic bag and
placed inside a box. Then the box is dated,
sealed, and stacked in a carton to be shipped.
In just one day, four thousand toy cars were
made at the factory.

At the end of each line is an *inspector* who checks the quality of the toys. She opens some boxes and looks at the toys to be sure that nothing is broken or missing. It is her job to see that broken toys DO NOT leave the factory!

The factory workers are always busy, making toys for children. Some work during the day. Others work at night. In one corner of the factory, space creatures are being made.

The arms and legs were made in a molding factory across the country. Before they're assembled, all parts must be inspected. Damaged parts hold up production on the assembly line.

Workers glue arms and legs to the bodies.
Clamps hold the bodies in place. It takes only
three minutes for the glue to dry, but workers
must keep going. While the glue is drying on
one space creature, another one is being made.

A scary green monster is put together on
another assembly line. Its long, creepy claws
and two extra legs are attached with a
clamping machine. The machine acts like a
stapler to attach the limbs to the body.

One creature's head was made in China, its body in the U.S.A. Once it is assembled, the rib cage is tested to see if it opens and closes. Does it work?

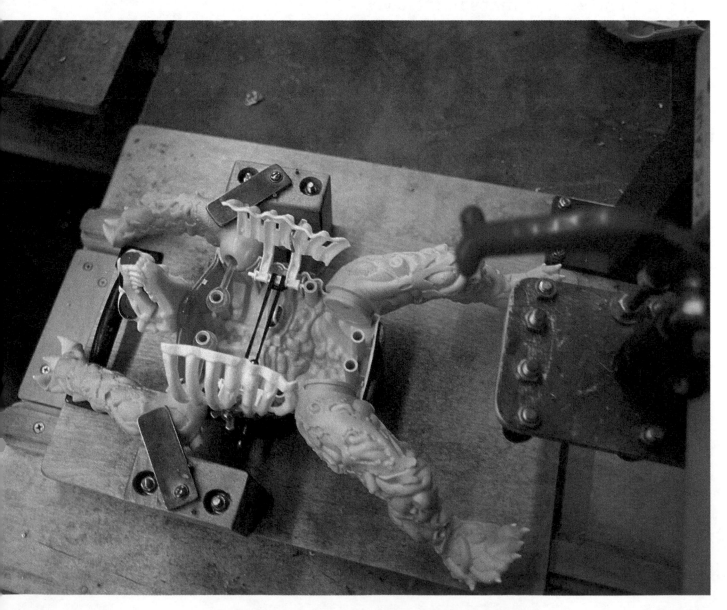

It does! The creature is tied to the back of its box so it will not break in shipping. Soon it's on to the toy stores. It is carried by truck or train.

The *manager* keeps track of things that happen at the factory. Are assembly lines running smoothly? Do workers have the parts they need? Are finished toys going out on time? The manager must know!

Cartons of finished toys are piled high in the loading area. Fork-lift drivers must load them into trucks that back up to the doors. From the factory warehouse it's on to the warehouse of the toy store itself.

Trucks deliver toys to the stores almost every day. The toy stores try to keep their shelves filled, especially when the holidays roll around!

Then children can pick out the perfect present for a brother or a sister. Or, mothers and fathers can buy the perfect present just for you!

Now that you know how some toys are made,
there is just one thing left to discover—how
much fun a toy can be when it's your very own!

St:M